SAINTS OF THE ROMAN CANON

by Julien Chilcott-Monk

*All booklets are published thanks to the
generous support of the members of the
Catholic Truth Society*

CATHOLIC TRUTH SOCIETY

PUBLISHERS TO THE HOLY SEE

TABLE OF CONTENTS

All rights reserved. First published 2013 by The Incorporated Catholic Truth Society, 40-46 Harleyford Road London SE11 5AY Tel: 020 7640 0042 Fax: 020 7640 0046. © 2013 The Incorporated Catholic Truth Society. Quotations and extracts from the Holy Bible are taken from The Jerusalem Bible *(1966)*

ISBN 978 1 86082 862 1

INTRODUCTION

To help us pray the Roman Canon, the First Eucharistic Prayer, it is useful to know a little about the prayers it contains, and particularly about the saints mentioned either side of the Consecration. It is of enormous benefit to us in our worship if we hold in our minds some knowledge of these holy men and women. Although they are, of course, representative of all saints and martyrs in all ages - indeed, both lists conclude with the words *et omnibus sanctis tuis* (*and all your saints*) - each saint mentioned is a signpost to aid us on our spiritual way; his or her special attributes can guide and encourage us on our journey through life.

The *Communicantes* (*In communion with*) prayer lists Our Lady, St Joseph and twelve apostles followed by a further twelve martyrs - popes, theologians and other faithful Christians. After the Consecration, in the *Nobis quoque peccatoribus* (*To us, also, your servants, who, though sinners*) prayer we have, after St John the Baptist, the later apostles and other martyrs, both men and women. These martyrs are all largely Roman martyrs, martyrs linked in some way with Rome, or martyrs particularly venerated in Rome, which is hardly surprising as we are dealing with the Roman Canon of the Roman Mass. They were well-known witnesses from a vast and ever-growing pool of saints. The history of the Roman Canon is a long and complicated one, and is not clear in all its details. These lists of saints have undergone some changes and amplifications over time, according to the varied traditions of particular churches, but the names as we have them now have been settled since the time of Pope St Pius V, and can be traced back, for the most part, perhaps as early as the fifth century. One exception is the addition of St Joseph by Blessed John XXIII. More recently, the identity of the John at the beginning of the *Nobis quoque* list has been clarified with the addition in vernacular translations of the words "the Baptist".

Devotion to the saints began exclusively with the martyrs - those who lost their lives on account of their steadfastness in the faith. Gradually saintliness was seen to embrace the confessors of the faith, those who lived a heroic life for Christ, and those who suffered hardship (whether self-imposed or not) for Christ.

On hearing the names of particular saints in the Roman Canon we celebrate what we know of them - their characters, their characteristics, and circumstances of their martyrdom. Those, and there are some, whose lives and passions have now largely been forgotten, are celebrated because their contemporaries - fellow Christians and, sometimes, even pagan enemies - acclaimed their sacrifice and resolution in the face of torture and death, and we can thus hold in our minds, along with the better-known saints, all those whose examples and sacrifices are now little known or forgotten. In some cases, where there are doubts as to the identity of a particular saint, the possibilities are considered carefully.

In praying the saints of the Roman Canon, we can use in our contemplation whatever knowledge we have of them - their strengths, weaknesses, circumstances of their martyrdom, their names, their ages and positions in life. In knowing something of them and holding these themes in our minds, we are much better equipped to pray the Canon.

After each biography, a comment and verses of an ancient hymn are added as aids to contemplation, and an idea or two for prayer, should the reader wish to make more of this pilgrimage through the lives and examples of the saints of the Roman Canon.

...FIRST OF THE GLORIOUS, EVER VIRGIN MARY, MOTHER OF OUR GOD AND LORD JESUS CHRIST...

8 December, 2 February, 25 March, 31 May,
15 August, 8 September etc.

Our Blessed Lady is here as the first among the saints; indeed, she is the Queen of the Saints. Her title *Mother of God* (*Theotokos or God-bearer*) was declared and confirmed at the Council of Ephesus in 431. By the very mention of her name, we are reminded of the great power of God to turn our preconceptions and prejudices upside down, as St Luke records in the words of the Magnificat. The tradition that Luke collected much from Our Lady herself is supported by this and the many other episodes in her life and in the early life of our Lord that he records.

At the Annunciation (25 March), the angel Gabriel (*God is my strength*) confronts Mary with her role in God's plan, a role to which she consents unequivocally. She would indeed be the bearer of God himself as he entered humanity. The angel prefaces the exchange with the salutation "Rejoice, so highly favoured! The Lord is with you!" (*Lk* 1:28) (the *RSV* translation has the more familiar "Hail, full of grace"). Thereby God declares through his messenger that Mary has, from her very conception, been chosen for this special vocation, but first she must agree to this terrifying responsibility. Her selfless response is simply "let what you said be done to me." (*Lk* 1:38) She is declared "highly favoured" or "full of grace" and so (we might put it) has already received the graces showered upon the baptised in the sacrament of Baptism. She is already free from the stain and burden of original sin - that sin of pride which places self before God. Mary's Immaculate Conception (8 December, and, consequently, the Feast of her Nativity celebrated on 8 September) is as much a necessary part of God's plan as is Mary's consent.

We celebrate Mary's calling upon her middle-aged cousin, Elizabeth, at the Visitation (31 May); her Purification at the Presentation of our Lord in the Temple (2 February) and we consider her seven great sorrows (15 September) predicted there by Simeon (*Lk* 2:22). By degrees those sorrows increase in intensity as she fulfils her promise. First, we have Simeon's prediction itself, and then the flight into Egypt, and the loss of our Lord in Jerusalem. His Passion is the fourth sorrow, followed by our Lady's standing at the foot of the cross, the descent from the cross and, finally, the burial in the tomb. Mary's commitment to her promise to God is absolute. Picture the scenes.

Mary and Joseph leave the temple and there in the precinct is an aged man, perhaps a permanent feature; he might have had the reputation for being slightly odd. However, he is here, his words divinely inspired to deliver the first of Mary's testing sorrows: "...and a sword will pierce your own soul too" (*Lk* 2:35). The second is the flight into Egypt, that frightening journey undertaken in order to protect the child Jesus from the murderous soldiers, those agents of the paranoiac King Herod the Great (40-c.4 BC), following the visit of the Wise Men. The disappearance of Our Lord as a boy during the expedition to Jerusalem is no less traumatic for his mother than the loss of a child would be today; Mary was presumably gripped with a feeling of devastation and utter panic. Throughout Jesus's later ministry the tension mounts culminating in the trials and final sentence, and the following of that sorrowful procession along the Via Dolorosa. Mary endures the mocking of her Son by the crowds as he hangs upon the cross and sees him die there. She sees his body lowered from the cross through her tear-filled eyes, and she is there as it is placed in the tomb. Throughout, Mary remains steadfast, trusting in God; but the sorrows are still sorrows, nonetheless.

How would our faith stand up to such testing situations? Would not a fraction of those sorrows break us? Yes, but for God's mercy and sanctifying grace so freely given to strengthen and to heal.

The joy of the Resurrection felt by Mary on that first day of the week we can understand and share because we live in that joy day by day. Sadly, we sometimes take it for granted, but the Holy Presence in the Most Blessed Sacrament restores us week by week. And so, Our Lady's task draws to a close, and that precious life, the faithful servant and Mother of God, is translated body and soul to the Heavenly Realms (15 August).

The God whom earth, and sea, and sky,
Adore and laud and magnify,
Who o'er their threefold fabric reigns,
The Virgin's spotless womb contains.

The God whose will by moon and sun
And all things in due course is done,
Is borne upon a Maiden's breast,
By fullest heavenly grace possessed.

How blest that Mother, in whose shrine
The great Artificer Divine,
Whose hand contains the earth and sky,
Vouchsafed, as in his ark, to lie!

(Quem terra, Pontus, aethera, ninth century, tr. J M Neale)

Pray for those who remain steadfast; for all religious.
Pray for us, O Holy Mother of God.

…BLESSED JOSEPH, HER SPOUSE…

Devotion to St Joseph is not a modern phenomenon, though it was not until the sixteenth century that the whole of the Universal Church began to celebrate a feast day in his honour. We know very little of his life but, notwithstanding, he stands before us as a distinct figure, strong, silent, dedicated, *upright* (as some translations have it - others say "righteous"), not too proud to obey the promptings of the Holy Spirit, which he does on at least three occasions as recorded in St Matthew's gospel. He is Spouse of our Lady and Guardian of God incarnate. (19 March) He is troubled about Mary's pregnancy (*Mt* 1:18f), receives Divine reassurance and then takes her as "his wife" (*Mt* 1:24). The bond of marriage is thereby confirmed. Joseph carefully protects Mary with her ever-growing Son within, as they travel to Bethlehem at the behest of the "authorities". It would have been no simple journey from Nazareth, cross country and down the eastern side of the Jordan, and eventually across to Bethlehem, a few miles due south of Jerusalem. Failure to make this journey would, presumably, have resulted in a severe penalty.

They are, perhaps, accommodated in the stable of an "innkeeper" - the owner of a collection of mean dwelling huts for travellers. This stable may well have been in fact an old-fashioned, indigenous, iron-age style house, lacking any Roman influence, with a few animals on the ground floor and family living-quarters on a mezzanine. There Mary would be given a bed and, maybe, a small sheep's manger was brought up from below, alongside her bedding, because there was no suitable cot and no other place for her baby.

We may imagine Joseph willingly carrying the manger up the ladder-like stairway to Mary's bedside, perhaps examining its construction as he does so. Afterwards, the Circumcision must be arranged and the journey to Jerusalem for the Purification and Presentation must be made. Foreign strangers - merchants, perhaps - visit them now, just as shepherds did before. All the time Joseph is vigilant. Now for the second time he responds to the Holy Spirit's promptings and the Holy Family flee along the coast to the Jewish community in eastern Egypt. Sometime later, when Herod the Great is dead, Joseph returns to the Holy Land and to Nazareth where he settles and provides for his family, working as a craftsman and carpenter (Joseph the Worker 1 May). He is well known at the beginning of Jesus's ministry but we hear no more of him as the ministry progresses.

Some traditions have made Joseph an old man at the time of his marriage to Mary; but there is no particular reason to think this, and he is also often shown as a vigorous man in the prime of life. Joseph was added to the *Communicantes* list at the end of the pontificate of Blessed John XXIII.

Are we dependable as Christians? Do we respond to the promptings of the Holy Spirit even if we are urged into the unknown?

Joseph observes the world in slow motion as the Heavenly Father's plan for the birth of his Son for a moment or two causes the whole of creation to stall, and then almost stand still.

Joseph went forth to seek a midwife in the village of Bethlehem.

"But as I was going" said Joseph "I looked up into the air, and I saw the clouds astonished, and the fowls of the air stopping in the midst of their flight. And as I looked down towards the earth, I saw a table spread, with farm workers sitting around it, but their hands were upon the table and they did not move to take food. They who had meat in their mouths did not eat. They who lifted their hands up to their heads did not draw them back: and they who lifted them up to their mouths did not put anything in; but all their faces were fixed upwards."

(Protevangelium of James)

Pray for all those who work selflessly for their families.

O Spouse of Mary, pray for us.

…YOUR BLESSED APOSTLES AND MARTYRS, PETER AND PAUL…

29 June & 22 February

Simon, whom our Lord nicknamed *Cephas* (*Peter*), the *Rock*, was a successful fisherman in Bethsaida. He was married and lived with his wife and mother-in-law in what might have been a sizeable house, perhaps (in the manner of the times) with a courtyard and separate kitchens. We might speculate that he was a junior partner in Zebedee's business, which employed many fishermen including his brother, Andrew, and the sons of Zebedee, James and John. With these two brothers, he seems to form an inner circle within the twelve, as together they witness the key moments in Jesus's ministry.

Was Jesus's nickname for Simon a little gentle fun? After all, Simon was known to be volatile, to be bold, courageous but sometimes unthinking - not exactly a rock upon which a Church could be built. But this is God's way, not ours. He turns impossible situations into something quite different; he converts the questionable into good; this we can see throughout the Old Testament and the New.

Simon Peter clearly possesses the qualities Jesus is looking for - boldness and determination. But first, those characteristics have to be tamed and controlled throughout the course of Jesus's ministry. "But who do you say that I am?" Jesus asks his disciples, and it is Simon Peter who blurts out "The Christ of God" (*Lk* 9:20). And in the gospel of Matthew, he declares "You are the Christ...the Son of the living God". Jesus replies "You are Peter and on this rock I will build my Church" (*Mt* 16:17, 18). So far, so good; later, however, Peter remonstrates with Jesus: "God forbid, Lord! This shall never happen to you". "Get behind me, Satan! You are an obstacle in my path..." (*Mt* 16:22, 23). Satan is the obstructer, he who tries to place obstacles between us and God. He is rather clever at making us do this work for him, and, often, do it unthinkingly or even willingly. But Peter's woes are not yet over, his bitterest pill is not swallowed until the last moment. "I will never lose faith" Peter declares. "Before the cock crows, you will have disowned me three times" Our Lord replies (*Mt* 26:33, 34). And of course, a little later, Peter does precisely what Jesus predicts. On hearing the crowing of the morning cockerel, "he went outside and wept bitterly" (*Mt* 26:75). All of us, in some way or another, have our *Peter* moments, do we not?

And Peter's training continued to the very end. Doubtless the other disciples were very grateful to Peter for expressing the doubts they had, the convictions they had, because it is always good to leave that sort of thing to others in case the idiot in oneself is laid bare for all to see. Peter's boldness and emphatic determination were the qualities, properly controlled, that the early Church would so desperately require.

Peter must have been well known to Jesus before his three-year ministry began; Andrew too. After all, their fellow-workers, James and John, were cousins of our Lord. It was just that, until John the Baptist pointed out to Andrew that Jesus was the one they ought to follow, they had not quite seen Jesus in that light. So often we need to be nudged in the right direction.

Our Lord was able to use St Peter as an example throughout his ministry: his reactions to circumstances and what was said were invaluable teaching aids; and his strengths and weaknesses were essential ingredients in the instruction of the others. Only after this sometimes gruelling apprenticeship could Peter stand with his fellow apostles and preach with utter confidence and conviction: "Men of Judaea, and all you who live in Jerusalem, make no mistake about this, but listen carefully to what I say... God raised this man Jesus to life, and all of us are witnesses to that...For this reason the whole House of Israel can be certain that God has made this Jesus whom you crucified both Lord and Christ" (*Ac* 2:14f).

The Rock upon which the Church was built disappears from Luke's account of the early Church in the Acts of the Apostles with the words "Then he left and went to another place" (*Ac* 12:17). He does, however, make a brief appearance at the Council meeting in Jerusalem (*Ac* 15:6). It is probable that he founded the Church at Corinth and then travelled to Rome to continue his work, where he was eventually imprisoned and subsequently crucified during the reign of Emperor Nero (54-68), in about 64. In Rome, according to tradition, he wrote the epistle we know as his first. There is a tradition that Mark's gospel was the fruit of his association with Peter in Rome. Peter and Paul are celebrated together on 29 June and the Feast of St Peter's Chair occurs on the 22 February.

> *Good Shepherd, Peter, unto whom the charge was given*
> *To close or open ways of pilgrimage to heaven,*
> *In sin's hard bondage held may we have grace to know*
> *The full remission thou wast granted to bestow.*

(Aurea luce, sixth century, tr. T A Lacey)

Pray for those who deny what they really believe;
> *pray for all fishermen. Pray for the Pope.*
St Peter, pray for us.

...AND PAUL, ANDREW...

29 June & 25 January

Saul of Tarsus was a Roman citizen and a Jew of the Pharisee party, an informant against Christians and a notorious persecutor of Christians; he was an enthusiastic witness to the stoning of Stephen, the first martyr. It was this man who became the apostle Paul in that hugely dramatic scene painted by Luke in the Acts of the Apostles (*Ac* 9:1f). Yet another example of God's choosing, in man's terms, an unlikely candidate for his own divine purposes, in order to call a worthy servant from a most dangerous man. And this transformed man began to preach about Christ but was ill received by those of the Church in Jerusalem who saw him as a dangerous spy. Eventually, St Barnabas was able to persuade them otherwise and accompanied Paul on his first missionary journey. At the end of this journey, Paul engaged in a rather unseemly dispute with Peter as the Church's attitude to converted Jews and to converted pagans was only slowly evolving. This is recorded in his letter to the Galatians (*Ga* 2:11-14). Whether or not good relations between them were ever restored is not known but it is likely that they were. Matters can rarely progress without rifts, disagreements and, finally, resolutions.

Paul was a prodigious traveller and writer of letters. He had a good command of language and, indeed, was well-read. The development of his theological thought can be discerned if his letters are read chronologically and not in the order we find them in the New Testament. A few of the letters attributed to Paul were probably neither written nor dictated by him but, nevertheless, might reasonably be described as "of his school". He suffered at the hands of the "authorities" in many places on his missionary journeys and these are listed ruefully in his second letter to the Corinthians (*2 Co* 11:22-29). He was, however, a courageous and undaunted missionary who cared for the embryonic churches throughout the Mediterranean and by his written and spoken encouragement helped them maintain their faith against overwhelming odds. His days ended in Rome, beheaded (a form of execution reserved for Roman citizens), a few years after St Peter's crucifixion in the reign of the emperor Nero (54-68). St Paul's Outside-the-Walls was built over his tomb by Pope Leo the Great (440-461).

Peter and Paul have long been honoured together and are celebrated jointly on 29 June. They are two sides of a coin, opposites in character, the former blazing a trail around the Mediterranean to Rome and the latter, through his letters, becoming, in one sense, the father of Christian theology and thought. His extraordinary conversion is celebrated separately on 25 January.

Why do we not pursue our God-given vocations with such zealous enthusiasm and ardour?

O noble teacher, Paul, we trust to learn of thee
Both earthly converse and the flight of ecstasy;
Till from the fading truths that now we know in part
We pass to fullness of delight for mind and heart.

(Aurea luce, sixth century, tr. T A Lacey)

Pray for all preachers and teachers; for all who risk their lives
*   for the Gospel.*
St Paul, pray for us.

…AND PAUL, ANDREW, JAMES…

A patron of both Russia and Scotland, Andrew, the brother of Peter, and employed by, or a partner in, Zebedee's successful fishing business at Bethsaida, was at first a disciple of John the Baptist. It was the Baptist who pointed Andrew, and another disciple, in the direction of Jesus, with the words "Look, there is the Lamb of God" (*Jn* 1:16). The two disciples then spent the day with Jesus. Different though this account is from the synoptic accounts of the call of the disciples, it need not conflict with them. Both Andrew and his brother would have been well known to Jesus, as his first cousins, James and John, were employed in the same fishing business. Up to this point, Andrew had never looked upon Jesus as the "Lamb of God" so naturally he would wish to spend some time talking to Jesus about the Baptist's strange assertion. The next day, Andrew told his brother "We have found the Messiah". Only later, we might suggest, when Jesus was ready to gather his disciples did he meet them beside the Sea of Galilee with the words "Follow me, and I will make you fishers of men" (*Mt* 4:19). There is nothing there that insists this must be a first meeting, only the first recorded in the gospel of Matthew.

In John's account of the miracle of the loaves, it is Andrew who informs our Lord "There is a small boy here with five barley loaves and two fish". He adds, rather doubtfully perhaps, that they are a very meagre starting point. Andrew is aware that Jesus knows precisely what will happen though he himself is still mystified. Is Andrew simply amusing everyone by pointing out the smallest person with the most modest provisions? No, Andrew is perceptive and is being helpful; he is collaborating with the work of God. He has already experienced the extraordinary miracle at Cana; he now has a quiet faith in the Lord's ability to change situations. As he points to the boy's rations, perhaps the boy himself decides to offer his food for the generous Creator's blessing - we may think it unlikely the food was summarily taken from him - and so the banquet is prepared.

When Andrew enables the boy to offer his food is he, perhaps, saying to our Lord "Obviously, these rations will not fill us, so how will you cause them to be sufficient for our needs, as I know you will?" In precisely this way our prayer and intercession can begin with openness of heart and faith in God's power. Our faltering requests and suggestions may be unprepossessing, but the transforming power of God responds to the smallest act of faith.

If we, in faith, hold others in our prayers and intercessions, is there ever a limit to God's bountiful goodness and transforming power?

The eternal gifts of Christ the King,
The Apostles' glorious deeds we sing;
And while due hymns of praise we pay,
Our thankful hearts cast grief away.

The Church in these her princes boasts,
These victor chiefs of warrior hosts;
The soldiers of the heavenly hall,
The lights that rose on earth for all.

(Aeterna Christi munera, 1st millennium, tr. J M Neale)

Pray for those who introduce others to the Faith;
*   for all catechists.*
St Andrew, pray for us.

...ANDREW, JAMES, JOHN, THOMAS...

25 July

James, the brother of John and son of Zebedee, was probably the elder of the two brothers and the driving force behind the request "Lord, do you want us to call down fire from heaven to burn them up?" when our Lord found a Samaritan village inhospitable (*Lk* 9:5ff). This occurred towards the end of Jesus's ministry; perhaps another incident gave rise to Jesus's nickname for the two brothers, "Boanerges" - the sons of thunder. They were, we might think, generally boisterous, fun-loving brothers - John egged on by James, probably. Jesus's nickname for the brothers - he clearly liked giving witty nicknames to his disciples - might be better rendered *The Thunder Boys*. Notwithstanding this jollity, James and John were highly thought of by Jesus. They were, together with Peter, his "inner circle" of disciples, who accompanied him on his most significant missions - from the raising of Jairus's daughter (*Mk* 5:35-43; *Lk* 8:49-56) to the time they are asked to be close to our Lord in his agony in the Garden of Gethsemane (*Mk* 14:32-42; *Mt* 26:36-46). These three were also together as witnesses of the Transfiguration as recorded in the three synoptic gospels.

Whether or not James remained in Jerusalem after Pentecost is not clear. There are a number of traditions associating him with Spain and he is, of course, the Patron of Pilgrims. However, it is likely that he was in Jerusalem preaching and teaching, and generally attracting attention, because King Herod Agrippa (37-44) was able to arrest and behead him with ease when he began to persecute "certain members of the Church" (*Ac* 12:1-3). James was thus the first apostle to be martyred.

Is it likely that our enthusiasm for the Faith would ever be sufficient to attract such opposition?

In these the Father's glory shone;
In these the will of God the Son;
In these exults the Holy Ghost;
Through these rejoice the heavenly host.

Redeemer, hear us of thy love,
That, with this glorious band above,
Hereafter, of thine endless grace,
Thy servants also may have place.

(Aeterna Christi munera, 1st millennium, tr. J M Neale)

Pray for pilgrims and those who seek Christ.
St James, pray for us.

…JAMES, JOHN, THOMAS…

27 December

John, and his brother, James the Great, were members of what might be described as our Lord's "inner circle" along with Peter. John was one of the "Boanerges" brothers (*Mk* 3:17) but, possibly, the less assertive of the two. It may be that he was the younger and that, because of his brother's strong influence over him, his mother asked Our Lord especially to look after John throughout his ministry. If John is to be identified with "the beloved disciple" or "the disciple Jesus loved" - that anonymous disciple, source of and influence behind the fourth gospel - this arrangement would fit. If so, John is likely to have been exceedingly embarrassed when he and James were marched before Jesus by their mother in a demand for special favours in the kingdom to come (*Mt* 20:20-24). Perhaps, from that point, his natural modesty overcame him and influenced the reminiscences that were the core of the gospel which bears his name.

Along with James and Peter, John attended significant events in Our Lord's ministry including the Transfiguration (recorded in the three synoptic gospels) and the final Agony in the Garden of Gethsemane (*Mk* 13:32-42; *Mt* 26:36-46).

In John's account of the dialogue from the cross with Jesus and Our Lady, we have perhaps the clearest example of dutiful discipleship. John accepts Jesus's command to take care of Mary as his own mother. At this point John takes on a grander role - he now seems to represent us, the Church, with Mary the Mother of the Church. We are bidden to honour her as Mother of the Church and to obey the commands of Jesus.

Legend tells us John was the only apostle not to be martyred and that he lived to a great age. Indeed, tradition makes Polycarp and Ignatius two of his devoted disciples.

How do others see the Church if we are her representatives?

To thee, Christ triumphing upon the cross,
In charge his holy Mother did commit,
That to the virgin thou, thyself her nephew,
With filial care should'st minister protection.

To thee the most high Father doth reveal
His word of prophecy, denied to others,
Do thou, O John, belov'd of our Lord,
Commend us all to God, in never ending prayer!

(Sequence for the Feast of St John from the Sarum Missal)

Pray for all those who help in encouraging devotion to Our Lady.
St John, pray for us.

...JOHN, THOMAS, JAMES...

3 June

Thomas comes from an Aramaic word meaning *twin*; this is why he is sometimes called the *twin* or, in Greek, *Didymus*.

All four gospels list Thomas as one of the twelve disciples, but Thomas's significant contributions, that comment upon Jesus's words and elicit important responses from him, are recorded only in the gospel of St John.

When Thomas and the other disciples hear from Jesus that Lazarus is dead, he suggests to the others that they should "...go too, and die with him" (*Jn* 11:16). Whose death is in his mind; Lazarus's? Hardly: he has just been declared dead. Is Thomas looking toward the end of Jesus's ministry? Does he see the storm clouds gathering and that the bringing back to life of Lazarus will further anger the scribes and Pharisees, and the temple officials? We cannot necessarily credit Thomas with such foresight but we know that Jesus had by this time identified himself as "the good shepherd...who lays down his life for his sheep" (*Jn* 10:11). Thomas clearly desires to stay with Jesus whatever happens. At this stage he sees himself as joining Jesus in death.

Later, after the Last Supper, Peter says "Lord, where are you going?" (*Jn* 13:36f). Jesus replies "Where I am going you cannot follow me now..." But Thomas cannot help himself: a little later (after the prediction of Peter's denial), his frustration mounting, perhaps, he interrupts Jesus. Jesus has just stated "You know the way to the place where I am going". Thomas asks Jesus to speak plainly and unequivocally. "Lord," he says, "we do not know where you are going, so how can we know the way?" Jesus replies: "I am the Way, the Truth and the Life" (*Jn* 14:4f).

After the Resurrection and after Jesus has appeared to the other disciples, Thomas refuses to believe when his fellows tell him "We have seen the Lord" unless he can feel the crucifixion marks on Jesus's body (*Jn* 20:24f). Why can he not accept his fellows' testimony? Is it simply that he obstinately requires physical evidence, and will believe or not believe when he has been able to assess its quality? Or, maybe, he has to contain his ecstatic joy, not *daring* to believe in case it is all a cruel dream. Perhaps he is profoundly upset that he was absent from the room. Perhaps he is simply willing Our Lord to repeat his appearance. And Jesus does appear to the disciples again; this time Thomas is present and he is invited to reassure himself. He does so and Jesus encourages all those not blessed with such an appearance with the words "Happy are those who have not seen and yet believe". However, before Jesus utters these words, Thomas acknowledges that he has touched both Jesus and God, thus affirming the true Divinity of Christ.

Our duty as Christians is to reveal to others Jesus Christ, true God and true man.

There is a long-established tradition that St Thomas
evangelised India.

Thy wounds before their eyes displayed
They see in living light arrayed,
And that they see they testify
In open witness fearlessly.

O Christ, the King of gentleness,
Our several hearts do thou possess,
That we may render all our days
Thy meed of thankfulness and praise.

(Sermone blando Angelus, fifth century, tr. T A Lacey)

Pray for those who lack faith.
St Thomas, pray for us.

...THOMAS, JAMES, PHILIP...

3 May

James, the son of Alphaeus (and maybe brother of Matthew, whose father also had the name of Alphaeus, if we adopt the traditional identification of Matthew with the Levi named in *Mk* 2:14), occupies the same position in each of the four lists of the Twelve (*Mt* 10:2-4; *Mk* 3:16-19; *Lk* 6:14-16; *Ac* 1:13). Paul might possibly be citing this James (usually called James the Less) in First Corinthians (*1 Co* 15:7) "...then he appeared to James, and then to all the apostles".

James the Less might have been leader of the Church in Jerusalem, though most assign this position to yet another James, known as James the Just (or James "the brother of the Lord"). This third James, the Just, is likely to have been the writer of the Epistle of James. We know almost nothing certain about James son of Alphaeus.

According to tradition, James the Less was martyred in 61 or 62, perhaps by stoning or being beaten with a club.

It is likely that the apostles Philip and James are celebrated on the same day simply because their relics were enshrined in Rome within a church dedicated to both.

O God, thy soldiers' crown and guard,
And their exceeding great reward;
From all transgressions set us free,
Sing thy Apostle's victory.

We therefore pray thee, full of love,
Regard us from thy throne above;
On this Apostle's triumph day,
Wash every stain of sin away.

(Deus, tuorum militum, sixth century, tr. J M Neale)

Pray for all organisers and administrators.
St James, pray for us.

...JAMES, PHILIP, BARTHOLOMEW...

3 May

Tradition has it that after Pentecost, the apostle Philip preached in Phrygia, particularly at the city of Hierapolis, where there was a substantial Jewish colony. Here he was martyred, possibly with his two daughters, but little else is known of him and the manner of his death.

His name is Greek and he himself may have been of Greek descent. He, like Peter, Andrew, James and John, lived in the town of Bethsaida, which, at the time, was something more than just a fishing village. Galilee, generally, was cosmopolitan and many Greeks and other nationalities had settled there.

"The next day, after Jesus had decided to leave for Galilee, he met Philip and said, 'Follow me'" (*Jn* 1:43-51). Subsequently, Philip was responsible for recruiting Nathanael (also known as Bartholomew).

Philip features in three important passages in the gospel of John. Jesus asks him before the miracle of the loaves, "Where can we buy some bread for these people to eat?" Philip is nonplussed. "Two hundred denarii would only give them enough for a small piece each". Even though he, presumably, attended the wedding in Cana, the possibility of any sort of miracle is not on his mind. Thomas helps an awkward situation by changing the subject and by pointing to the boy's absurdly meagre provisions. To these two statements, Jesus responds "Make the people sit down". Money is not necessary in this case; the Heavenly Father will provide. The boy's offering is sufficient; there is no need to seek a solution elsewhere, the answer is here (*Jn* 6:1-15).

Later, "Some Greeks...approached Philip... 'Sir, we should like to see Jesus'". We would *see* Jesus - that is, we would understand him, be enlightened by him. In this sign that the world is beginning to focus on him, Jesus sees the commencement of his "hour" - his time. And he now responds to Philip's request, to Andrew and, presumably, the Greeks: "Now the hour has come for the Son of Man to be glorified. Only if the grain dies in the soil will it yield a rich harvest," he explains. This surely is the time when that grain must fall to the ground and die (*Jn* 12:20-25).

It is because of Philip's honest question to Jesus during the evening of the Last Supper, "Lord, let us see the Father and then we shall be satisfied", that Jesus finally is able to reveal himself to the disciples, and remove all doubt. "Have I been with you all this time, Philip...and you still do not know me?" "To have seen me is to have seen the Father...I am in the Father and the Father is in me..." (*Jn* 14:8-12).

Let us be grateful to Philip for having the courage to ask the questions we do not have the courage to ask.

In these the Father's glory shone;
In these the will of God the Son;
In these exults the Holy Ghost;
Through these rejoice the heavenly host.

Redeemer, hear us of thy love,
That, with this glorious band above,
Hereafter, of thine endless grace,
Thy servants also may have place.

(Aeterna Christi munera, 1st millennium, tr. J M Neale)

Pray for those who convey Christ to others.
St Philip, pray for us.

...PHILIP, BARTHOLOMEW, MATTHEW...

24 August

Bartholomew was possibly Nathanael's surname - it means the Son of Tolmai. He is likely to be the acquaintance of Philip in the gospel of John. The association of Bartholomew's name with Philip's in the synoptic gospels suggests that Bartholomew and Nathanael are one and the same, a disciple of our Lord and one of the Twelve. The name Bartholomew appears in the lists of the Twelve (in *Mt* 10:2-4, *Mk* 3:16-19, and *Lk* 6:14-16); and in John, Philip introduces Nathanael from Cana in Galilee to our Lord. First, Philip tells Nathanael "We have found the one Moses wrote about in the Law...he is Jesus, son of Joseph, from Nazareth". "From Nazareth?" asks Nathanael, perhaps with a grin. And we can imagine his emphasising "can any good come out of that place?" "Come and see," Philip suggests. Philip and Nathanael approach Jesus who sees them coming and remarks of Nathanael straight away: "There is an Israelite who deserves the name, incapable of deceit". Can we imagine Nathanael, with a huge grin on his face, asking "How do you know me?" "I saw you under the fig tree". In mock obeisance, perhaps, Nathanael replies: "Rabbi, you *are* the Son of God..." "Ah!" says Jesus "You will see greater things than that!" (*Jn* 1:43-51).

Surrounding the story of Bartholomew are many legends describing his tireless missionary work in many countries; he is generally credited with the conversion of Armenia, perhaps in the company of St Jude. Bartholomew was martyred, according to legend, after converting the King of Armenia, whereupon the king's brother immediately had Bartholomew beheaded. Bartholomew died, legend tells us, in the city of Albanopolis. One story says he was flayed - hence his patronage of tanners.

A cheerful countenance is much more likely to reveal Christ to others.

Then let the earth, the courts of heaven, applaud,
The Church here present add her acclamations,
The Apostles' high and holy acts extolling.

These are the candlesticks before our God;
These in the palace of the mighty King
Exalted sit, in place aloft.

Salt of the earth, light of the world are they
Like heavenly luminaries they shine;
These bear the palm, these wear the crown,
Already for them was the table set.

(Sequence for an apostle, from the Sarum Missal)

Pray for those who use wit to good effect;
*   for all comedians and actors.*
St Bartholomew, pray for us.

...BARTHOLOMEW, MATTHEW, SIMON...

21 September

Levi seems to have been renamed Matthew - *a gift of The Lord* - by Jesus himself, perhaps so that he might dissociate himself from his former life. According to Mark 2:14, Levi was the son of Alphaeus and thus, quite possibly, the brother of James (*see above*).

Matthew was a tax-gatherer for the Roman authorities, and would therefore have been considered a sinner by the scribes and Pharisees and, indeed, generally reviled by Jews and non-Roman Gentiles alike.

In both the gospels of Mark and Luke, Matthew is referred to as Levi, but in the gospel of Matthew, he is named Matthew from the moment he appears.

Jesus crosses the water in a boat and alights at Capernaum, his own town, where he heals a paralytic. He declares the man's sins forgiven, and then instructs him to "Get up, and pick up your bed and go off home" after some of the people question his power or authority to forgive sin. Afterwards, he sees Matthew (or Levi) in the custom-house and says "Follow me". Matthew responds immediately. He too has sins to be forgiven and he has, we can surmise, sat at his post mulling this over maybe for years. Was he awaiting the divine nudge? Later, perhaps the same day, a number of tax-gatherers join Jesus, and, presumably, Matthew, at dinner. Was Matthew's sudden conversion such an attractive idea to them that they simply had to discover more? How many of them joined the outer ranks of Jesus's disciples (*Mt* 9:1-13)?

From the earliest times, Matthew has been associated with the gospel that carries his name. Of course, there is no firm evidence for this attribution, though long-held tradition is persuasive. It is likely, in any event, that between the time of the Fall of Jerusalem in AD 70 and the year 80, this gospel achieved its present form. Its ingredients are drawn from a source known to Luke and, it is probable, from Mark's gospel. However, its starting point could have been a collection of reminiscences by the hand of Matthew himself, maybe in Hebrew or Aramaic, aimed at the Jewish reader.

Many traditions claim Matthew as a visiting missionary in this place or that. His most likely area of interest, after Pentecost, was Judaea itself, and then, perhaps further east. The manner of his death is not known.

Matthew shows us how we ought to react to divine promptings.

O Saviour Jesu, not alone
We plead for help before thy throne;
Thy Mother's love shall aid our prayer
To win for us that healing care.

Let all who served thy Church below,
And now thy heavenly freedom know,
Give heed to help our lingering strife
And claim for us the crown of life.

(Jesu, Salvator saeculi, ninth century, tr. T A Lacey)

Pray for all writers of religious work, for study and devotion.
St Matthew, pray for us.

...MATTHEW, SIMON AND THADDEUS [JUDE]...

28 October

Perhaps it seems odd that the two apostles Simon and Thaddeus (Jude) are honoured on the same day: there is, however, a tradition to connect them - that they travelled together to Persia where they were martyred, after earlier and separate missionary journeys: Simon's to Egypt and Jude's to Syria. There are some conflicting stories about the two saints.

In the gospel of Luke, Simon is referred to as "Simon called the Zealot" (*Lk* 6:16); Matthew (*Mt* 10:4) and Mark (*Mk* 3:18) call him "the Canaanite" or "the Cananaean" though in *The Jerusalem Bible* this is also translated "the Zealot". Presumably the two expressions are roughly equivalent. "Zealot" was certainly a name associated with those who yearned for, and eventually instigated, an uprising against the Roman occupiers. If Simon was such a man, would he remain so after three years with Jesus? It is sometimes argued that Judas Iscariot was also of that mind, remained so throughout Jesus's ministry, and finally and misguidedly tried to precipitate an uprising. It can also be argued that "Zealot" could mean nothing more than zeal for the Law. Again, we might equally consider Simon's soubriquet as yet another of Jesus's affectionate nicknames. Perhaps Simon was an outspoken young man of some vigour whom Jesus dubbed "the Revolutionary".

We do not know. Simon suggests to us that we ought to
devote more of the energy of our enthusiasms to the work
of Christ.

Lord of Creation, bow thine ear, O Christ, to hear
The intercession of thy servant true and dear,
That we unworthy, who have trespassed in thy sight,
May live before thee where he dwells in glorious light.

O God our Saviour, look on thine inheritance,
Sealed by the favour shining from thy countenance;
That no false spirit bring to naught the souls of price
Bought by the merit of thy perfect sacrifice.

(Annue Christe, saeculorum Domine, 1st millennium,
    tr. T A Lacey)

Pray for those who work hard for peace and harmony.
St Simon, pray for us.

...SIMON, THADDEUS [JUDE]; LINUS...

28 October

Thaddeus, better known as Jude and most famous as the patron saint of lost causes, may have been Simon's companion in death. They are venerated on the same day.

There is some confusion over the individuals in the New Testament named Judas and James (*see above*). In the lists of the twelve disciples in the gospels and in the Acts of the Apostles, John's gospel records this disciple as "Judas, not Iscariot" (*Jn* 14:22); Luke gives us "Judas of James" (*Lk* 6:16), which some understand as "Judas, brother of James", and others "Judas, son of James". In both Matthew's gospel (*Mt* 10:3) and Mark's gospel (*Mk* 3:18), there is no second disciple named Judas; his place is occupied by Thaddeus, normally supposed to be another name for the same person. Some scholars like the idea of Jude as *brother* of James as that seems to support his authorship of the epistle in his name. The Epistle of Jude opens: "From Jude, servant of Jesus Christ and brother of James..." It is more likely that the superscription of the epistle merely cites James (perhaps James the Less, leader of the Church in Jerusalem) as a "brother *in Christ*". To add to the doubt, some more recent opinions date the epistle of Jude to a time after the likely lifespan of the apostle.

However, there is a very important contribution made by Jude and recorded in the gospel of John. Sounding a little frustrated, he makes a penetrating observation, and brings forth from Jesus words that reveal something of the mystery of the Holy Trinity, the three Persons of God.

> Judas - this was not Judas Iscariot - said to him, "Lord, what is all this about? Do you intend to show yourself to us and not to the world?" Jesus replied: "If anyone loves me he will keep my word, and my Father will love him, and we shall come to him...the Advocate, the Holy Spirit, whom the Father will send in my name, will teach you everything and remind you of all I have said to you."

"If anyone loves me he will keep my word". Thus by loving Christ, we are keeping his word; we keep his word by loving him. From loving him, everything else flows.

Thank God for the perception of Jude in eliciting one of our Lord's most important discourses.

> *We bear the burden of our guilt and enmity,*
> *Until thy pardon lift the heart from slavery;*
> *Then through the spending of thy life-blood, King of grace,*
> *Grant us unending triumph in thy holy place.*

> *To thee the glorious Christ, our Saviour manifest,*
> *All wreaths victorious, praise and worship be addressed,*
> *Whom with the living Father humbly we adore,*
> *And the life-giving Spirit, God for evermore.*

> (Annue Christe, saeculorum Domine, 1st millennium,
>   tr. T A Lacey)

Pray for all those who are depressed and suffer mental breakdown; those who can turn to no one.

St Jude, pray for us.

…THADDEUS [JUDE]; LINUS, CLETUS…

23 September

Regarded as the second pope (counting Peter as the first), Linus reigned, if such a term can in any way be assigned to the incumbency of these early bishops, for a decade or so. Early Church historians place him as Bishop of Rome at a period between 56 and 81. It is certainly not unlikely that he died a martyr, but of such an event there is no evidence, apart from tradition. Most ancient traditions do not spring from nothing. The responsibility of overseeing the embryonic Church of Rome was no mean task. At any moment, one's life could be demanded. Linus may well have followed Peter and Paul in martyrdom. His name was included in the Roman Canon and he was venerated as a martyr.

He may well have been the Linus mentioned at the conclusion of Paul's second letter to Timothy: "Greetings to you from Eubulus, Pudens, Linus, Claudia, and all the brothers. The Lord be with your spirit. Grace be with you."

Our duty is always to be prepared to be called to witness to Christ in difficult and dangerous conditions.

O Thou, of shepherds Prince and Head,
Now on a Bishop's festal-day
Thy flock to many a shrine have sped
Their vows to pay.

He to the high and dreadful throne
Urged by no false inspiring, pressed,
Nor on hot daring of his own,
But Thy behest.

And so, that soldier good and tried,
From the full horn of heavenly grace,
Thy Spirit did anoint, to guide
Thy ransomed race.

(Christe Pastorum, tr. Blessed J H Newman)

Pray for those who take up the challenge and work to
promote the Catholic Faith.
St Linus, pray for us.

...LINUS, CLETUS, CLEMENT...

26 April

Anacletus (usually shortened to Cletus) was probably Greek, and of humble stock. Traditionally, he followed Linus as Bishop of Rome and died in a persecution in the late first century, perhaps during the reign of the emperor Domitian (81-96). Apart from his place in the Roman Canon, and a reputation as a martyr, we know practically nothing about him.

Let us consider, for a moment, life for the Christian during Domitian's persecutions.

And he became a father true,
Spending and spent, when troubles fall,
A pattern and a servant too,
All things to all.

His pleading sets the sinner free,
He soothes the sick, he lifts the low,
Powerful in word, deep teacher, he,
To quell the foe.

Grant us, O Christ, his prayers above,
And grace below to sing thy praise,
The Father's power, the Spirit's love,
Now and Always.

(Christe Pastorum, tr. Blessed J H Newman)

Pray for those who guide the Church; for all Cardinals.
St Cletus, pray for us.

...CLETUS, CLEMENT, SIXTUS...

23 November

Clement succeeded Cletus in about 91 and remained as Bishop of Rome for about ten years. Like Linus and Cletus, he was considered a martyr and placed in the Roman Canon. But there is no reliable information or early tradition about his martyrdom.

It is marginally possible that he is the Clement cited in Paul's epistle to the Philippians (usually dated to the mid-50s). "These women were a help to me when I was fighting to defend the Good News - and so, at the same time, were Clement and the others who worked with me. Their names are written in the book of life" (*Ph* 4:3).

Clement was the author of a *Letter to the Corinthians* written at a time when the Church in Corinth was in turmoil. In earlier centuries this letter was included in the New Testament canon.

"Let us, therefore, humble ourselves, brethren, laying aside all pride, and boasting, and foolishness, and anger: And let us do as it is written.

For thus says the Holy Spirit; 'Let not the wise man glory in his wisdom, nor the strong man in his strength, nor the rich man in his riches; but let him that glories, glory in the Lord, to seek him and to do judgement and justice.'

Above all, remembering the words of the Lord Jesus, which he spoke concerning equity and long-suffering, saying, 'Be merciful and you shall obtain mercy; forgive, and you shall be forgiven...' by these rules, let us establish ourselves, that so we may always walk obediently in his holy words; being humble minded" (Clement 7:1-5).

Thou gem of prelates, such the boon we crave
With meet devotion, and with minds sincere,
Instantly for thy favour making prayer,
That we may pass beyond the sacred threshold,
And, standing there within the lofty place,
Find joyful welcome in that joyful realm.

In this thy court we, holy prelate, wait,
And with great joy and festal jubilee
Sing now our sweet and heightened lays.

(Sequence for a Prelate from the Sarum Missal)

Pray for all bishops, priests and deacons and administrators of dioceses.

St Clement, pray for us.

...CLEMENT, SIXTUS, CORNELIUS...

7 August

This is probably not Pope Sixtus (more correctly, Xystus - a Greek name) I, traditionally the seventh pope, who reigned from about 116-125. Instead, it is more likely to be Pope Sixtus II. His short reign - from 257 to 258 - was insignificant compared with his generous and holy martyrdom. Sixtus II succeeded Pope Stephen I at a time when the emperor Valerian (253-260) was beginning his determined persecution of the Church. In his short reign, Sixtus II managed to restore good relations with Cyprian, Bishop of Carthage (*see below*), who had bitterly disagreed with Pope Stephen I, although the issue over which they had disagreed was not resolved until some time after the deaths of all three.

The manner of the deaths of St Sixtus and his saintly companions, as described in legend, was remarkable. Sixtus was about to preach. He sat, flanked by his deacons (who are usually named as Agapitus, Felicissimus, Januarius, Vincent, Magnus and Stephen). When a detachment of the Imperial Guard entered the church, the deacons under Sixtus's direction remained calm and still, patient and stubbornly unresisting, so that the congregation could disperse and leave unmolested. This apparently riled the soldiers so much that instead of arresting Sixtus and his deacons, as they had been ordered to do, they killed them on the spot. Some accounts suggest that St Felicissimus and St Agapitus were killed later on the same day.

Let us sit for a moment with St Sixtus and contemplate.

O God of the soldiers the Portion and Crown,
Spare Thy people, who hymn the praise of the Blest;
Earth's bitter joys, its lures and its frown,
He scanned them and scorned, and so is at rest.

Thy Martyr he ran all valiantly o'er
A highway of blood for the prize thou hast given.

We kneel at Thy feet, and meekly implore,
That our pardon may wait on his triumph in heaven

(Deus tuorum militum, sixth century, tr. Blessed
     J H Newman)

Pray for all those who place the welfare of those in their care
*   first at the expense of their own wellbeing and comfort.*
St Sixtus, pray for us.

...SIXTUS, CORNELIUS, CYPRIAN...

16 September

Cornelius, of a distinguished Roman family (the *gens Cornelia*), was pope between 251 and 253. After his election, the priest Novatian (antipope 251-258) contrived to have himself consecrated bishop in order to oppose Cornelius. Cornelius was supported by Cyprian, Bishop of Carthage (whose feast is celebrated jointly with Cornelius), and Dionysius of Alexandria, and armed with this support, convened a synod in Italy of some sixty bishops for the purpose of confirming his legitimacy. He received the endorsement he required: Novatian and his followers were excommunicated.

One of the bones of contention was whether full communion should be restored to those who had apostasised during the persecutions of the emperor Decius (249-251). Novatian argued that none should be readmitted to the fold, but Cornelius, Cyprian and the supporting bishops took a more moderate view. Important correspondence between Cornelius and Cyprian, on this matter and others, is extant.

At the end of the reign of the emperor Trebonianus Gallus (251-253), a fresh wave of persecution of Christians began. Pope Cornelius was condemned and exiled to Civita Vecchia where he suffered many privations. Cyprian supported him in prayer and correspondence. It is probable that Cornelius died in exile as a result of those privations, although a later tradition speaks of his subsequent trial, imprisonment and beheading. In either case, he would be reckoned a martyr and Cyprian often spoke of him as such.

Let us reflect on our constancy under pressure and threat.

On champions blest, in Jesus' name,
Short be your strife, your triumphs full,
Till every heart have caught your flame,
And lightened of the world's misrule
Ye soar those elder Saints to meet,
Gathered long since at Jesus' feet,
No world of passions to destroy,
Your prayers and struggles o'er, your task all praise and joy.

(The Christian Year, John Keble)

Pray for senior clergy and bishops who are challenged by those who advocate unorthodox ways.
St Cornelius, pray for us.

...CORNELIUS, CYPRIAN, LAWRENCE...

16 September

Cyprian is believed to have been born in about 200, in Carthage, during a time when the Church was growing fast. After a successful and notable career in public service, in oratory, and in advocacy, Cyprian was converted largely by what he discerned in an elderly priest, one Caecilius. Following his baptism - when over the age of forty - he was ordained priest and soon afterwards elected bishop, an honour he tried to resist. He became Bishop of Carthage in 248. His deacon, Pontus, records that, as bishop, Cyprian was highly thought of and much respected for his humility, skill and gentleness.

Under the emperor Decius (249-251), all Christians in Carthage and elsewhere were ordered to offer sacrifice to the pagan gods. This, of course, was a recurring theme as emperor succeeded emperor. Many Christians, faced with dire threats of what would befall anyone failing to comply, apostasised. Cyprian, now in hiding, administered his diocese through correspondence.

In the dispute which raged in Rome on the matter of the readmission of apostates, Cyprian supported Pope St Cornelius (*see above*) as he himself leniently readmitted such people after prescribing a short time of penance.

In an edict promulgated in 257, the emperor Valerian demanded specifically that Christian clergy sacrifice to the pagan gods. Cyprian was, at first, exiled for his refusal to comply and then rearrested and returned to Carthage. There he seems to have been retried and sentenced to death. In all probability he was stabbed in the neck or beheaded.

Cyprian, a Father of the Church, has left us a large body of important theological writing.

In his treatise on the approach of death and martyrdom, Cyprian writes: "...laying aside our fear of death, think only on the following immortality. In this way, let us show that we are what we believe...let us be happy in the day...that frees us from the snares of the world, and restores us to the kingdom of heaven." "Martyrdom is a baptism...which, as we leave the world, immediately binds us to God."

God is to be admired in His Saints,
Who by His grace wrought great and wondrous acts:
Who by the excellency of their faith
Subdued the world and its most grievous ills;
The threatening of the judges, cruel stripes,
And blandishments, with steadfast soul despising,
They for their King poured out their souls to death.

(Sequence, Common of Martyrs, from the Sarum Missal)

Pray for prelates who maintain their faith and uphold their duties to their flocks despite threats of violence and sanctions.
St Cyprian, pray for us.

...CYPRIAN, LAWRENCE, CHRYSOGONUS...

10 August

St Lawrence was one of the Roman deacons who perished with Pope Sixtus II (*see above*). The story of his death that has come down to us has been developed and elaborated over the centuries.

We are again in the reign of the emperor Valerian (253-260). As the story goes, for some reason, Lawrence was absent from Sixtus's side. He was later apprehended and taken before the emperor. The emperor, who is represented as knowing something about the responsibilities of deacons, orders Lawrence to return with the valuables of the Church. Lawrence is given three days, during which he sells everything of value. He gives the money to the poor, and returns to the emperor's court in the company of the wretched and deformed, and presents them as the Church's valuables. Inevitably, this taken as a grave insult to the person and position of the emperor and Lawrence is sentenced to death: not, as was usual, death by beheading, but a slow and painful death by roasting on a grille over a fire. This famous story may not be historical, but, one way or another, St Lawrence was martyred for Christ.

The story does give us pause for thought, however. The poor, the weak, the neglected are indeed the treasures of the Church; Jesus himself looks out from their eyes as, indeed, he shines from our own faces when we minister to them.

With the victor's laurel crownéd, now they triumph -
Christ's holy footsteps duly following,
That spotless Lamb, to whom unceasing
They pour forth sweetest hymns, fulfilled with grace.

May Christ, who is our glory, grant that we
Who celebrate the feast today
May be found meet to be with them above.

(Sequence, Common of Martyrs, from the Sarum Missal)

Pray for those who serve the Church with honesty and diligence; those who are unswerving in their faith.

St Lawrence, pray for us.

...LAWRENCE, CHRYSOGONUS, JOHN AND PAUL...

24 November

Very little is known about Chrysogonus, his life and his martyrdom. All that seems certain is that he was martyred in the city of Aquileia, on the banks of the river Natissa, during the persecutions of the emperor Diocletian (284-305). One source makes Chrysogonus spiritual adviser to Anastasia (*see below*), but the connection is not certain, and is in some ways unlikely. In the absence of any other detail, it is most probable that Chrysogonus was beheaded for refusing to abandon his faith and make sacrifice to pagan gods.

What is beyond doubt is that Chrysogonus is well known to our Heavenly father.

> *Lo sweetly sounds the deep-toned Alleluia,*
> *Closing the Martyr's glorious requiem.*
> *The blessed angel radiant host stands round*
> *In triumph, crying, Holy! Holy! Holy!*
>
> *In the Apostles' brilliant habitation,*
> *Judging all peoples, nations, languages,*
> *Enthronéd high, a shining company,*
> *Who counted all the pomp of life as dross;*
> *Like stars they glitter in the firmament.*

(Sequence, Common of Martyrs, from the Sarum Missal)

Pray for those who are adamant against the tide of secularism.
St Chrysogonus, pray for us.

...CHRYSOGONUS, JOHN & PAUL, COSMAS & DAMIAN...

26 June

John and Paul cannot be identified with any certainty. One story makes them brothers, perhaps former soldiers, who worked in the service of the family of the emperor Constantine. When Julian II (Julian the Apostate) became emperor in 360, he ordered a resumption of the worship of the old pagan gods and (so the story goes) had the brothers killed for their wilful disobedience.

Whatever the truth of this, there is good evidence that relics of these two martyrs were placed in the house given by Pammachius on the Caelian Hill (one of the Seven Hills of Rome) where a church was subsequently built and dedicated to the brothers. Remains of an early dwelling house containing their shrine have been found beneath the foundations of the later basilica.

We honour all martyrs for their steadfastness in face of pain and death. Let these holy martyrs represent all those other martyrs now long forgotten.

Now in the heavenly kingdom they have place,
Most excellently uttering triumphant words,
Or chanting forth their hymns of exultation -
With skill to praise attuned,

And voice of accent sweet -
To Christ their king, bowing submissively.

(Sequence, Common of Martyrs, from the Sarum Missal)

Pray for soldiers and domestic staff; all those who serve others honestly and faithfully.

St John and St Paul, pray for us.

...JOHN & PAUL, COSMAS & DAMIAN, AND ALL YOUR SAINTS...

26 September

Cosmas and Damian met their deaths probably at Cyrrhus, to the north of Antioch, although other traditions give Cilicia. Their dates are not known, although they may have been killed during the infamous persecutions of the emperor Diocletian (284-305). Later legend, which however commands little historical value, says they practised medicine as itinerant doctors without demanding any payment, with joy and dedication in accordance with Jesus's commands.

Their names were early associated with those of Roman martyrs; Pope Symmachus (498-514) encouraged the devotion.

When we consider the pain we suffer on account of our minor sacrifices, do we feel ashamed?

Clothed in white robes the Martyrs make them ready,
Warriors who fought the battle of the world.
Lo, with white coronets the saints are crowned
Who witnessed righteously with good confession,
And lying words disdained,
Contending for the faith;
Now in the heavenly kingdom they have place.

(Sequence, Common of Martyrs, from the Sarum Missal)

Pray for those who practise medicine and those who care for others without ever seeking reward.

St Cosmas and St Damian, pray for us.

...YOUR HOLY APOSTLES AND MARTYRS: WITH JOHN THE BAPTIST, STEPHEN...

24 June & 29 August

It was not until the Roman Canon was translated into the vernacular languages in the late 1960s that the John of the *Nobis quoque* list was unequivocally identified as John *the Baptist*. Most had thought him to be so. After all, John the apostle is clearly the John in the *Communicantes* list before the Consecration. And, indeed, this is the position John the Baptist enjoys in some earlier rites.

John was one of Jesus's cousins; as we remember, as soon as Mary heard of Elizabeth's pregnancy, she rushed to Judaea to greet her. Even before his birth, John was set apart as a man of especial holiness, filled with God's spirit.

Apart from Our Lady, John the Baptist is the only saint whose earthly and heavenly birthdays we celebrate - an honour that underlines the importance of his role. We know nothing about his early life. Some have speculated that he was he an Essene, living and learning in the desert community at Qumran, and have also suggested that Jesus studied there too. However, all we are told in the gospel is

In due course John the Baptist appeared; he preached in the wilderness of Judaea and this was his message: "Repent, for the kingdom of heaven is close at hand." This was the man the prophet Isaiah spoke of when he said: "A voice cries in the wilderness: prepare a way for the Lord, make his paths straight." This man John wore a garment made of camel-hair with a leather belt round his waist, and his food was locusts and wild honey. (*Mt* 3:1-4)

Matthew's gospel pictures John as a wild and hairy figure - an Elijah-like man - roughly hewn and roughly-dressed. He was down-to-earth in his preaching without doubt. "But when he saw a number of Pharisees and Sadducees coming for baptism he said to them, 'Brood of vipers, who warned you to fly from the retribution that is coming?'" (*Mt* 3:7) And yet, he drew great crowds and baptised all those who from "Jerusalem and all Judaea and the whole Jordan district made their way to him" (*Mt* 3:5).

John was the forerunner, "the man the prophet Isaiah spoke of". He was to plant a message in peoples' minds, humbly dismissing his importance: "the one who follows me is more powerful than I am" (*Mt* 3:11). He prepares them with a baptism of repentance: he aims to increase their awareness; he aims to make them ready. At the appropriate time, John was able to point Andrew, one of his disciples, in the right direction - towards Jesus, and say "Look there is the Lamb of God" (*Jn* 1:35-36). And so, John bows off the stage leaving room for God's plan to unfold further.

A wild man and an Old Testament figure? Yes, of course, but perhaps there is also something of the desert father, and of a thirteenth century friar about him. He has turned the last page of the Old Testament and closed the age of the prophets and has opened the beginning of the New.

Although he is the last of the prophets of old, he is also the epitome of the selfless saint and martyr.

Are we able to allow the spotlight to fall on others?

The holy Baptist's yearly fest,
Herald of Christ, we celebrate:
Whose life and conversation follow;
Most holy man, thou friend of Jesus,
Devoutly now we share your joys,
Which, unto Zacharias, Gabriel promised
To those who thy nativity do keep;
That through this feast may rejoice for ever,
Where happy saints of God unite.

(Sequence for the Feast of John the Baptist, from the Sarum Missal)

Pray for those whose vocation it is to prepare for others.
St John the Baptist, pray for us.

...JOHN THE BAPTIST, STEPHEN, MATTHIAS...

26 December

Luke paints a colourful and three-dimensional picture of this man, the proto-martyr, in the Acts of the Apostles. Stephen was the first of seven deacons ordained by the apostles to assist them by caring for the less fortunate among both Hebrew and Greek Jews, of whom Stephen was one. He assisted also with preaching and teaching and soon gained a reputation as a marvellous orator and worker of miracles.

Stephen spoke with vigour and authority, so much so that the authorities conspired to have witnesses declare "We heard him using blasphemous language against Moses and against God" (*Ac* 6:11). He was arrested and taken before the Sanhedrin. Perjurers made the case against him. In response to the allegations, Stephen launched into the most eloquent and beautifully crafted history of Israel and her relationship with God. He showed how, at every turn, Israel had consistently disobeyed and rejected God's commands and love. Stephen skilfully reaches the conclusion of his summary: "You stubborn people, with your pagan hearts and pagan ears. You are always resisting the Holy Spirit, just as your ancestors used to do. Can you name a single prophet your ancestors never persecuted? In the past, they killed those who foretold the coming of the Just One, and now you have become his betrayers, his murderers." Afterwards, the council "rushed at him, sent him out of the city and stoned him" (*Ac* 7:51-58). Stephen's clothes (his mantle, perhaps?) were laid at the feet of one Saul, a young man and persecutor of the Church. No one then knew that Saul would wear that mantle with pride.

We might dwell upon Stephen's fearlessness and confidence in the Lord.

Saint of God, elect and precious,
Protomartyr, Stephen bright
With thy love of amplest measure,
Shining round thee like a light;
Who to God commendedst, dying,
Them that did thee all despite.

Glitters now the crown above thee,
Figured in thy sacred name:
O that we, who truly love thee,
May have portion in the same;
In the dreaded day of judgement
Fearing neither sin nor shame.

(Sancte Dei pretiose, 1st millennium, tr. J M Neale)

Pray for all missionaries and missionary organisations.
St Stephen, pray for us.

...STEPHEN, MATTHIAS, BARNABAS...

14 May

Peter instructs the other apostles that they must restore the number twelve by appointing a man to take the place vacated by Judas Iscariot. He instructs them that the man must be one who could testify to the Resurrection, who had travelled with them throughout Jesus's ministry. It is not unlikely that the two candidates were from the seventy-two disciples sent out to preach by Our Lord.

Having nominated two candidates, Joseph, known as Barsabbas, whose surname was Justus, and Matthias, they prayed, "Lord...show us which of these two you have chosen..." They drew lots for them, and as the lot fell to Matthias, he was listed as one of the twelve apostles (*Ac* 1:23-26).

Little is known about St Matthias - many legends abound as to the places his mission took him; the most probable being Judaea and Cappadocia. There is a tradition that has him stoned to death in Jerusalem. Though we know so little, those who elected him knew him well. Indeed, he had been in their company for three years. The apostles would have known everything there was to know about him and they already held him in high regard. What else do we need to know?

Let the round world with songs rejoice;
Let heaven return with joyful voice;
All mindful of the Apostles' fame,
Let heaven and earth their praise proclaim.

Ye servants who once bore the light
Of Gospel truth o'er heathen night,
Still may your work that light impart,
To glad our eyes and cheer our heart.

(Exultet caelum laudibus, c. tenth century tr. R Mant)

Pray for all those who are elected to office that they may remain true.

St Matthias, pray for us.

...MATTHIAS, BARNABAS, IGNATIUS...

11 June

Barnabas (termed *apostle* by Luke) was a Cypriot who generously sold the land he owned and placed it in the fund that the early Church held in common. He was chosen to carry the gospel and the news of Stephen's martyrdom to Antioch. He took St Paul as his companion. It was a journey and mission to be undertaken only by someone with a suitable temperament. After all, Paul was new to the followers of Christ and, indeed, had been their enthusiastic persecutor and a supporting bystander at St Stephen's death. Barnabas and Paul met with success at Antioch. "As things turned out they were to live together in that church a whole year, instructing a large number of people. It was at Antioch that the disciples were first called 'Christians'" (*Ac* 11:27). On later journeys, he was accompanied by John Mark. Legend tells us Barnabas was stoned to death in Salamis, where he was buried.

A cheerful disposition goes hand in hand with a Christian life.

For at thy will they preached the word
Which cured disease, which health conferred:
O may that healing power once more
Our souls to grace and health restore:

That when the Son again shall come,
And speak the world's unerring doom,
He may with them pronounce us blest,
And place us in thy endless rest.

(Exultet caelum laudibus, c. tenth century tr. R Mant)

Pray for those who give generously and cheerfully and for those who do not.

St Barnabas, pray for us.

...BARNABAS, IGNATIUS, ALEXANDER...

17 October

Ignatius of Antioch in Syria was martyred in Rome in or about the year 110 in a period of renewed persecution, during the reign of the emperor Trajan (98-117). Little is known save that he was Bishop of Antioch in Syria in 70. He is believed to have been a disciple - along with Polycarp - of the apostle John. Ignatius referred to himself as the God-carrier and exhorted his flock to understand that it was the vocation of a follower of Christ to bear God with him and thus reveal him to others.

Ignatius was condemned in Antioch and taken in chains on the long and arduous journey to Rome. Most of what is known about Ignatius is revealed in the seven letters he wrote or dictated and had delivered in the course of his journey.

The first four of his letters - those addressed to the Ephesians, Magnesians, Trallians and the Romans - were composed during a break in the journey at Smyrna. St Ignatius was apparently permitted visitors and many came to offer their support and prayers. And his letters to the Churches in Ephesus, Magnesia and Tralles were mostly letters of thanks and encouragement to keep faith in Christ. He was keen to hail the Ephesians as God-carriers, Christ-carriers, who carry holiness with them throughout their daily lives. He reminds the Magnesians that to be called a Christian means *being* a Christian. And he gives a gentle warning to the Trallians about the need to avoid heresy. He assures his friends and acquaintances in Rome that he has accepted his sentence and looks forward to his death as the door to life. He sees that death through suffering is a privilege. He is aware that he will become the food of ferocious beasts and that they will devour every scrap of him.

At the next station - at Troas - Ignatius writes to the Church in Philadelphia and Smyrna, and to the Bishop of Smyrna, Polycarp. He encourages them in their faith and greets them warmly and effusively. After this he travels further by sea and by land until he finally reaches Rome.

It was not long before he was flung to his death in the Flavian Amphitheatre in Rome, known to us as the Colosseum. There an assortment of hungry wild beasts consumed him for the entertainment of enthusiastic crowds.

Allow me to be the food for wild beasts of prey, which is the manner in which I shall make my way to God. God's wheat flour I am, and by the teeth of the beasts of prey I shall be ground that I may prove to be Christ's pure bread. Better still, encourage these beasts of prey to become my sarcophagus and to leave no part of my body behind: once I am at sleep, I have no wish to be a burden to anyone. Only at that time shall I be called a true disciple of Christ Jesus when the world can see nothing of me - not a scrap of my body. (*Letter to the Romans*)

May we, with Ignatian equanimity, face our wild beasts of prey.

Worthy deeds they wrought and wonders,
Worthy of the name they bore;
We with meetest praise and sweetest
Honour them for evermore.

Faith prevailing, hope unfailing,
Jesus loved with single heart -
Thus they glorious and victorious
Bravely bore the Martyr's part.

(Twelfth century hymn, translated in the 1861 Hymns
    Ancient and Modern)

Pray for all those who communicate the Faith in writing and
    face opposition with a smile and confidence in Christ.
St Ignatius, pray for us.

...IGNATIUS, ALEXANDER, MARCELLINUS...

3 May or 10 July

There has been much debate and confusion over the identity of this saint. Up to the early decades of the twentieth century, authorities, including Dr Adrian Fortescue in his book *The Mass*, were content to identify this Alexander with Pope Alexander I (109-116), even though he was not placed in sequence with the other popes in the *Communicantes* prayer. Now, however, it is believed that Pope Alexander was not martyred, nor was he buried, as it was supposed, on the Via Nomentana outside Rome.

More probably, the martyr named may be the Alexander who, along with six fellow Christians, refused to sacrifice to the pagan gods of Rome, and was consequently tortured and killed. This is supposed to have occurred in the time of emperor Antonius Pius (136-161). The story forms an obvious parallel to the story of the martyred Seven Brothers in the Book of Maccabees. According to legend, Alexander, Vitalis and Martial were beheaded; Januarius, Felix and Philip were thrashed to death; and Silvanus was thrown from a height and dashed to pieces. The feast day of these martyrs, in the pre-1969 calendar, is 10th July.

Another possible candidate is another Alexander, a martyr who was buried on the Via Nomentana. In 1855 an ancient tomb was discovered there, inscribed with the name Alexander. Is this our man? According to legend, he was a priest, and along with two fellow priests, Eventius and Theodulus, was tortured to death in an especially horrible way, during the reign of the emperor Hadrian (117-138). His feast is celebrated on 3rd May, which is also the feastday of Pope Alexander I; this might explain the misidentification mentioned above. Whoever Alexander was, it is probable that the name was added to the *Nobis quoque* list by Pope St Symmachus (498-514). We honour all martyred men with the name Alexander.

> *How wondrous is God in his doings, in his Saints and in the gifts he giveth them.*
> *By faith, they o'ercame temptations and the foes that beset their lives.*
> *Threats from judges, stripes, and wiles of flattery,*
> *All these they despise for the sake of the King of kings, shedding their life-blood willingly.*
> *Therefore they triumph, decked with the crown of victory,*
> *As those who follow the steps of Christ, who is the holy Lamb of God.*

(Sequence, Common of Martyrs, from the Sarum Missal)

Pray for all those of this name; for those who do not seek after other gods; for those who worship the fashionable idols. Pray for ourselves. St Alexander and Holy Companions, pray for us.

...ALEXANDER, MARCELLINUS, PETER, FELICITY...

2 June

Marcellinus was a priest in Rome; and Peter, in minor orders, was an exorcist. In common with so many martyrs, they suffered under the persecutions of the emperor Diocletian (284-305).

The account of their martyrdom is late and may not be reliable in its details. It says they were locked up and, while in prison, converted many to the faith including the gaoler and his family. Eventually, Marcellinus and Peter were together taken before a judge and sentenced to death. They were removed from their cell one night to be beheaded secretly and buried in the Silva Nigra, three miles or so outside the city; perhaps it was anticipated that the Christians of the city of Rome would make a public tomb a place of veneration and focus of attention. In the woods the men were first forced to dig their graves.

Their graves were found by two Christian women - Lucilla and Firmina. The executioner, it is said, was converted by the demeanour of his victims, and disclosed the whereabouts of the grave. The women recovered the bodies and had them buried more satisfactorily and respectfully in a catacomb close to the Via Labicana.

Even though this story may be fanciful in parts, there is strong evidence that Marcellinus and Peter were popularly venerated in the city of Rome. Later, the emperor Constantine (306-337) built a church over their tomb. He buried his mother St Helena in the church. In Pope Damasus's reign (366-384), the tomb of the two martyrs was further embellished.

The two saints revealed Christ to their executioner as they dug their graves.

> *For thee through many a woe they ran,*
> *In many a fight they played the man;*
> *For thee their blood they dared to pour,*
> *And thence have joy for evermore.*
>
> *We therefore pray thee, full of love,*
> *Regard us from thy throne above;*
> *On these thy Martyrs triumph day,*
> *Wash every stain of sin away.*

(Deus tuorum militum, sixth century, tr. P Dearmer)

Pray for all those who are abducted and imprisoned secretly. St Marcellinus and St Peter, pray for us.

...MARCELLINUS, PETER, FELICITY, PERPETUA, AGATHA...

7 March

In the year 203, in Carthage, during the persecution by the emperor Septimus Severus (193-211), many Christians were arrested. These included five catechumens - people under instruction in the faith who were not yet baptised: Vibia Perpetua, who was nursing a child, and was the wife of a Roman official; two slaves, Revocatus and Felicity, who was heavily pregnant; and two freedmen (ex-slaves), Saturninus and Secundulus. Another catechumen, Saturus, seems to have voluntarily accompanied them to the place where they were kept under house arrest.

Perpetua kept a journal of the days they spent there, and records their baptism. She describes their removal to a more horrible incarceration in a dark and dank prison. There she was visited by her pagan father, who begged her to sacrifice to the pagan gods for the wellbeing of the emperor, and so gain her release. She refused. Her father took her child away to look after it. Secundulus died in prison.

When their case came before the court at the Forum, they again confessed their Christianity and refused to sacrifice. The men were whipped and Felicity and Perpetua slapped repeatedly across their cheeks and brows. The judge then passed the sentence of death - death in the arena by means of the wild animals kept there for that purpose.

Perpetua's journal ends the day before they were taken to the arena. Felicity had, not long before, given slightly premature birth to her child, which meant her death in the arena would not be delayed. An unknown hand - perhaps the great writer Tertullian - completed the story.

Apparently many began to believe in Christ purely on account of the resignation, composure and faith of these condemned men and women.

On the day set for the "games", as they were euphemistically termed, the remaining five were led to the arena accompanied by the cheers and jeers of an expectant audience. This was all done for the entertainment of the local inhabitants, including soldiers stationed nearby.

First, Saturninus and Revocatus were attacked by a leopard and a bear; then Saturus was tied to a wild boar. After this, Felicity and Perpetua were bound to an angry heifer, goaded to the point of madness: both were soon thrown to the ground, badly bruised and only semi-conscious. As the games drew to a close, the crowd bayed for the Christians to hobble and crawl to the centre of the arena to allow clear sight of their deaths. The sword made short work of them.

These saints were much venerated in Rome.

How sorely are *we* tested?

Like sheep their blood they poured;
And without a groan or tear,
They bent before the sword
For that their King most dear:
Their souls, serenely blest,
In patience they possessed.

And looked in hope towards their rest.
What tongue may here declare,
Fancy or thought descry,
The joys thou dost prepare
For these thy Saints on high!

(Sanctorum meritis, eighth century, tr. J M Neale)

Pray for all who are threatened but still remain constant.
*Pray that we may show Christ to others simply by our
    general behaviour.*
St Felicity, St Perpetua and Holy Companions, pray for us.

...FELICITY, PERPETUA, AGATHA, LUCY...

5 February

Agatha was highly acclaimed and venerated for her unswerving faith and resolution. She became quite a cult figure in Rome in the fourth century and Pope Gregory the Great (590-604) probably added her name to the *Nobis quoque* list.

Traditions of the early virgin saints frequently merge and borrow from each other. The core of this story is that Agatha was a woman who lived in the Sicilian town of Catania, probably in or about the end of the third century, during the time of the persecuting emperor Diocletian (284-304). She was likely martyred during the Diocletianic persecution. The remaining details of the story cannot be taken as certain fact. Agatha, the story goes, was attractive and wealthy, and had dedicated her chastity and virginity to Christ. The local prefect ordered her to be brought before him on the pretext that she had espoused Christianity and refused to sacrifice to the local gods. He was struck by her beauty, and perhaps offered her freedom in exchange for sexual favours. She refused and was immediately sentenced, brutally tortured and martyred.

Do we daily break the promises we have made to Christ - whatever they are?

The pleasures of the world she spurned,
From sin's pernicious lures she turned;
She knew their joys imbued with gall;
And thus she reached thy heavenly hall.

We therefore pray thee, full of love,
Regard us from thy throne above;
On this thy martyr's triumph day,
Wash every stain of sin away.

(Deus tuorum militum, sixth century, tr. J M Neale)

Pray for those who ill-treat and exploit others.
St Agatha, pray for us.

...AGATHA, LUCY, AGNES...

13 December

Not unlike Agatha, Lucy was a Sicilian, but from the city of Syracuse rather than Catania. Like Agatha, she died during the reign of the emperor Diocletian (284-304) and very soon became a popular saint in the city of Rome and in many other cities.

Also like Agatha, most of what we know as her life-story was written much later and should not be thought of as strictly historical. The story states that she was dedicated to Christ and to the poor to whom she daily, willingly and freely gave of her wealth (which was considerable). Once, as she walked home after giving alms, she was assaulted by a Roman soldier, who tried to rape her. Lucy successfully resisted him and, out of spite, he denounced her to the authorities as a Christian. Lucy was arrested, tortured and either beheaded or stabbed in the neck.

The legend tells us that Lucy's eyes were especially beautiful. She is the patroness of those with eye injuries and disorders. Eyes, of course, bring light (the meaning of her name) to the body and to others. Doubtless the light of Christ himself shone from her eyes as she distributed her money among those less fortunate than herself.

So they passed through pain and sorrow
Till they sank in death to rest;
Earth's rejected, God's elected,
Gained a portion with the blest.

By contempt of worldly pleasures,
And by deeds of valour done,
They have reached the land of Angels,
And with them are knit in one.

(Translation unattributed)

Pray for all who are vulnerable to the authority and
*   influence of others.*
St Lucy, pray for us.

...LUCY, AGNES, CECILIA...

21 January

Agnes is another virgin martyr from the time of Diocletian. Like Agatha and Lucy, most details of her life are late and unreliable; the core of the story makes her a young woman who refused marriage because of her Christianity, and was martyred. Built over the place of her death is the church of Sant' Agnese in Agone, Rome. As in the cases of Agatha and Lucy, she very quickly became a much honoured saint in Rome.

The life and death of Agnes will bring to mind saints throughout the centuries who have dedicated their lives to Christ from an early age; those who have faced mockery and death unwaveringly, at the hands of the unscrupulous, merciless and powerful.

Jesu, the Virgins' Crown do thou
Accept us as in prayer we bow;
Born of that Virgin whom alone
The Mother and the Maid we own.

Amongst the lilies thou dost feed,
With Virgin choirs accompanied -
With glory decked, the spotless brides
Whose bridal gifts thy love provides.

(Iesu, Corona Virginum, St Ambrose, fourth century, tr. J M Neale)

Pray for prostitutes and those who are employed in other branches of the industry; pray for those who live and flourish at their expense.

St Agnes, pray for us.

...AGNES, CECILIA, ANASTASIA...

22 November

The identification of this virgin martyr is not without some difficulty. She may be an otherwise unknown martyr over whose house a church at Trastevere in Rome was erected as early as the third century. By the end of the fifth century, a church had been dedicated in her honour. However, the popular story (involving the conversion of her betrothed, Valerian, and his brother Tiburtius) seems to be no earlier than the fifth century. It may have been composed to explain the life of the unknown dedicatee of the church.

In this legendary biography, the men were condemned for their Christianity and for respectfully burying the bodies of Christian martyrs. They were beheaded along with Maximus, a Roman civil servant, who was converted by their example. Cecilia in turn buried their bodies and was then herself questioned and finally sentenced to death. Before she died, she made over the property to the pope (Pope Urban I, 220-230).

Pope Pascal I 817-824 had what he reckoned were the bodies of these four saints (Cecilia, Valerian, Tiburtius, Maximus) removed from the catacomb and translated to the church of St Cecilia where they remain. In the late sixteenth century, the supposed body of Cecilia was uncovered and before it succumbed to the atmosphere, the artist Moderno had made a detailed drawing on which his statue of Cecilia was subsequently modelled. This remarkable statue still lies in the church.

There was probably only ever one martyr by the name of Cecilia, who was associated in some way with the house that later became a church.

Cecilia is well-known as the patroness of musicians, and although this is probably based on a misunderstanding of a phrase in her biography, this does not seem to matter.

May the intercession of Cecilia and her companions instil in us unswerving dedication to Christ.

But now more steadfast do the virgins stand,
While tortures new are laid upon them,
Rejoicing that their bodies are afflicted
For everlasting glory, which they seek,
Seeing the joys of this world pass
And suddenly fade as flowers,
In such a virgin lot shone Cecilia,
As amidst lesser lights the day-star gleams.

Blest virgin, who didst bear all fearlessly,
And for that glory willingly didst die,
Devoutly intercede for us to God.

(Sequence, Common of Virgin Martyrs, from the Sarum Missal)

Pray for musicians, poets and artists.
St Cecilia, pray for us.

...CECILIA, ANASTASIA
AND ALL YOUR SAINTS...

25 December

Anastasia was probably martyred at the end of the reign of the emperor Diocletian (284-304). She was venerated in the city of Sirmium in the Roman province of Pannonia (now part of Serbia) where, in all probability, she lived and died. It is likely that she suffered the frequent fate for a Christian at this time and was arrested, imprisoned and killed. (A doubtful account connects St Anastasia to St Chrysogonus (*see above*) and has her travelling to Aquileia - where St Chrysogonus was martyred - to care for the poor and eventually be martyred.)

In the fifth century enthusiasm for this martyr reached Rome; at about the same time, St Anastasia's church in central Rome received its dedication. In fact, the church may have begun in a building owned by a woman called Anastasia, perhaps the emperor Constantine's sister, and interest in the martyr may have been sparked by the existing name of the building.

Let us honour the whole noble army of martyrs.

They, wheresoe'er thy footsteps bend,
With hymns and praises still attend;
In blessed troops they follow thee,
With dance and song and melody.

We pray thee therefore to bestow
Upon our senses here below
Thy grace, that so we may endure
From taint of all corruption, pure.

(Jesu, Corona Virginum, St Ambrose, fourth century, tr.
    J M Neale)

Pray for those who have lost their identity and are
unknown; for organisations dedicated to finding the lost
and the missing.
St Anastasia, pray for us.

FURTHER READING

Bentley, James *A Calendar of Saints* (1986)

Butler's Lives of the Saints, new edition (12 volumes, 1995-2000)

Chilcott-Monk, Julien *A Basic Dictionary of Bible People* (Canterbury Press, 2004)

Chilcott-Monk, Julien *A Calendar of Catholic Devotion* (Canterbury Press, 2008)

Fortescue, Adrian *The Mass - A Study of the Roman Liturgy* (1912)

Martyrologium Romanum (2005)

Milburn, R.L.P. *Saints and their Emblems in English Churches* (Basil Blackwell, 1961)

Oxford Dictionary of Popes, ed. Kelly, J.N.D. (2nd edition, 2010)

Oxford Dictionary of Saints, ed. Farmer (5th edition, 2011)

Penguin Dictionary of Saints edd. Attwater & John (3rd edition, 1995)

The Roman Martyrology (1961)

Saints of the Roman Calendar

Fr Nicholas Schofield

The Church sets aside special days throughout the year to remember particular saints with feasts, memorials and solemnities. From the best known reformers, founders and Doctors of the Church, to lesser known saints and martyrs, each has been carefully chosen by the Church to be celebrated for his or her life and works. These texts help us to discover more about these holy men and women and why they are so important. It is an invaluable tool for daily prayer and a helpful introduction to those who loved Christ in a special way.

This booklet includes brief biographies of all the saints of the new General Roman Calendar celebrated by the universal Church and those of the national calendars of Australia, England, Ireland, Scotland and Wales.

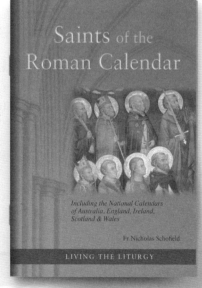

Saints of the Roman Calendar

Including the National Calendars of Australia, England, Ireland, Scotland & Wales

Fr Nicholas Schofield

LIVING THE LITURGY

B748   ISBN 978 1 86082 790 7

Doctors of the Church

Fr Jerome Bertram

The Doctors of the Church were saints who were devoted to the Word of God, eager to listen to the Holy Spirit, and to pass on to others what they had learned. Each memorable and influential figure is described in this intriguing booklet with a concise summary of their contribution to the Church and to the development of doctrine. Their preaching and writing continue to influence people today.

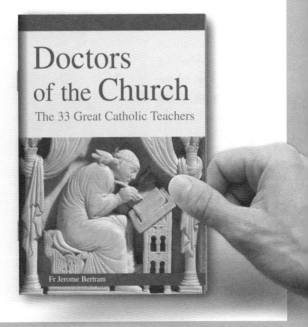

B742   ISBN 978 1 86082 746 4

A world of Catholic reading at your fingertips...

Catholic Faith, Life & Truth for all